W9-BVY-464

Twelve Faces of Grief

Text © 1998 by Charlie Walton
Published by One Caring Place
Abbey Press
St. Meinrad, Indiana 47577

Cover and interior design by Scott Wannemuehler

All rights reserved.
No part of this book may be used or reproduced
in any manner without written permission of the
publisher, except in the case of brief quotations
embodied in critical articles and reviews.

Library of Congress Catalog Number

98-73566

ISBN 0-87029-323-0

Printed in the United States of America

Twelve Faces of Grief

A Grief-Recovery Handbook for Group or Personal Use

by
Charlie Walton

ONE
CARING
PLACE

To

Jerry Porter,

friend of a lifetime

CONTENTS

PREFACE

The title *Twelve Faces of Grief* arises from the fact that this book has twelve chapters. It is not intended to suggest that there are twelve distinct or sequential stages of grief. That would be too simple. And anyone who has been through deep grief knows that there is nothing simple about it. You cannot reliably predict or anticipate all the stages.

It is possible to move through the stages like clockwork. Or all of the stages may hit you simultaneously. Stages will occur in a unique and personal order, and any stage may pop back up long after you thought you were finished with it.

Each of the twelve chapters of this

book introduces a single aspect of grief. The intent is for each chapter to facilitate (1) group discussion if the book is being used by a grief-support group, or (2) individual reflection if the book is being read alone.

The title of each chapter is expressed in the form of a quotation, a set of words that might typically fall from the lips of a person struggling through that chapter's aspect of grief. For example, the chapter entitled "There Must Be Some Mistake" introduces the denial that occurs at some point—or at many points—in any griever's struggle to process an unbelievable, unacceptable truth.

Each chapter begins with a Case Study, a fictitious but realistic story intended to focus our thinking on that chapter's topic. Some Case Studies are presented as first-person monologues. Others are third-person narrations. All describe problem situations resulting from some life tragedy. When used in a group setting, the Case Studies have been most effective when read aloud by a member or facilitator.

To foster group discussion, and to guide individual reflection, a short list of Discussion/Reflection Questions follows the Case Study in each chapter. Each question is intentionally worded in an open-ended fashion. These are not questions that are intended to elicit short answers; rather, the goal is wide and deep exploration through group discussion or individual reflection (or both). They have proven effective in generating useful and therapeutic discussions. In the hands of an experienced group facilitator, these questions can also be molded and adapted to speak to specific needs of individual group members.

Each chapter concludes with a few thoughts on the topic at hand. In some cases, these summary thoughts relate to previous Discussion Questions. More often, they present opinions and concepts that I have developed by means of a decade of conversations and interactions with grieving persons. In some cases, a group member or facilitator may find it useful to read this section aloud, as a summary to the group's discussion. In other cases, they will be more profitably shared in the natural progression of the group discussion, or read in the privacy of one's home. In every case, you should feel free to adapt the book to fit your group or personal needs. Use parts or the whole. Follow the book's sequence or create an order that meets your needs.

This book goes out with my prayer that it will ease the pain and increase the positive aspects of grief in all our lives.

Charlie Walton
April 1998

CHAPTER 1

"There Must Be Some Mistake."

(Denial)

CASE STUDY
The son who couldn't die

The night the policeman came to bring the bad news, Marvin laughed in his face. The policeman had never seen that response. He was delivering the news that Marvin's son, Chad, had been killed in a climbing accident. Marvin's first response was a spontaneous laugh. But then his face clouded over in anger. "Look, buddy," he said. "I don't know who put you up to this, but it's not funny. This is sick. And, if you're not really a cop, you're in trouble."

The policeman gently persisted,

showing Marvin his own identification and Chad's driver's license. Marvin's angry face melted into a vacant stare as he said, "There must be some mistake, Officer. My son teaches climbing. He teaches safe climbing. You've gotten that license off some other kid—maybe one of Chad's students. My son will be walking through that door any minute now, smiling and sweaty, and making a bee line for a hot shower."

When they took Marvin to identify Chad's body, he shook the boy and said, "Wake up, Chad. Time to get up, pal. Time to go home." At the funeral home, Marvin would stand by the coffin and tell visitors, "Look at him. Good lookin' kid, isn't he? Looks just like he's asleep."

In the months after the funeral, people were concerned about Marvin. It was hard to tell just where his mind was with regard to Chad's death. Most of the time, his responses were reasonable, and acknowledged the fact that Chad was gone. But if the conversation turned to

Chad, Marvin would leave the room. And whenever the door opened, Marvin would look up eagerly as if Chad had finally come home.

Even a year after Chad's death, Marvin continued his confusing, double-minded behavior. He did begin to use phrases like "before Chad left" and "since Chad is gone," but he still kept Chad's room exactly as the boy had left it. And whenever a car pulled into the driveway, Marvin would jump up, hurry to the window, and then turn back in disappointment when he saw that it wasn't Chad coming home.

Discussion/Reflection Questions

1. *How would you evaluate Marvin's reaction to Chad's death?*

2. *If you went to talk with Marvin, would you agree with him when he spoke of Chad still being alive? Would you think it better to gently nudge him toward acceptance of*

the truth? Or would you have some other strategy?

3. *Is Marvin working his way out of denial? Will the passage of time take care of Marvin's problem?*

4. *What difference do you think it might have made if Marvin's wife had been part of the story?*

5. *Have you ever had a terrible dream that seemed real? Can you relate that experience to Marvin's behavior in any way?*

6. *Describe a time when you (or someone you know) refused to believe some really bad news. In that case, what arguments did the mind give for refusing to accept the awful truth?*

7. *What connection can you see between adults in denial and children having imaginary playmates?*

8. *What are some of the "whistling in the dark" statements people make to deny traumatic situations?*

A few thoughts on DENIAL

When we think about the contortions our minds go through to protect us from overwhelming pain, it's easy to see the mind as a separate personality, as a faithful caretaker or servant always trying to make things easier for us. One psychologist told me, "Our minds always keep us mentally balanced, but some of the things they have us thinking in order to stay in balance may convince other people that we are loony tunes."

Denial is a natural process our minds put us through when we need extra time to process some new and unanticipated development. Nothing could be healthier than giving the mind the time and space it requires to work through some traumatic new thought, to cope with a sudden terrible new truth, to develop strategies for comfortably relating the truth of the past to the truth of the future.

Those gathered around in support may experience the greatest anxiety during a grieving person's periods of denial and readjustment. It is easy for supporters to become aggressive and push the griever to "snap out of it" and accept the harsh truth. It is much harder to match our timetables for recovery with the timetable of the one for whom the shock is happening firsthand.

Whatever the cause of the grief, those of us who are eager to help need to remind ourselves of something important. The time it takes an emotionally battered mind to readjust to a new reality is likely to be a whole lot longer than the time it takes for outside observers. Patience is not only a virtue, it is the only way to really help.

It is possible for persons to get stuck in denial and to require professional help to come to grips with a painful new truth. In some cases, the mind seems to assume that as long as the terrifying new reality is not put into words, the event has been prevented from becoming real. Usually the disbelief gradually diminishes, and when it re-occurs, it does so with lessened intensity. Nevertheless, years after someone you love dies in an accident, you may find yourself repeating, "There has to be some mistake. This cannot have happened. The chance of all those ifs coming together in the same event is almost mathematically impossible."

Disbelief and a certain amount of denial are natural and beneficial activities of the mind that allow us time to adjust to shocking information. They are sure signs that we are experiencing a life trauma. Those who wish to help us "get over denial" at this time need to back off just a bit, stop trying to control things, and let the human mind do its amazing protective work.

CHAPTER 2

"It's Just Not Fair."

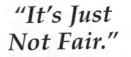

(Fairness)

CASE STUDY
The kick in the stomach

Susan had been employed at Rafferson Industries since she graduated from high school. Mr. Rafferson himself had hired her. Like most of her fellow employees, Susan idolized Mr. Rafferson. He was the most unselfish person any of them had ever known. He never made business decisions only for business reasons, and often spoke lovingly of "our little family of employees."

Susan came to think of Mr. Rafferson as her adopted father. She loved baby-sitting young Katie Rafferson, and often slept over to keep her company when the Raffersons had to go out of town to industry conferences.

Susan had been with the company 24 years, and was head of her division when the news came that the corporate jet had gone down in fog as the Raffersons returned from a meeting in Chicago. There were no survivors.

Susan's knees gave way. She had to be helped to the infirmary and later driven home. Everyone in town was saddened, but Susan was beyond sad. Her husband and children were sorry about the Raffersons, but they were more concerned for the wife and mother who could not get over the tragedy.

When the plant reopened after the funeral, Susan wandered about in a stupor. She would sit at her desk and stare into space. She would mumble, "It's not fair. It's just not fair. He was the kindest, most selfless man I ever knew. He didn't deserve to die. It's just not fair."

Susan couldn't make it through a

meeting without crying. Professional counseling had little effect. Months after the airplane crash, Susan remained virtually non-functional. Her husband, her children, and her coworkers were extremely concerned. It seemed as if Susan might never get over the death of the Raffersons, might never get past the terrible unfairness of it all.

Discussion/Reflection Questions

1. *How appropriate was Susan's behavior after the Raffersons' deaths?*

2. *If Susan's family members and work colleagues asked your advice, how might you advise them?*

3. *How do you feel about Susan's charge that the Raffersons' deaths were unfair?*

4. *Where do most of us get our rules about what is fair and what is unfair?*

5. *Are some kinds of grief "worse" than others? How do we measure grief?*

6. *How would you describe the relationship between frustration and grief?*

7. *If you are confident that something positive will eventually come from the grief your friend is suffering, how wise is it to tell your friend so?*

A few thoughts on FAIRNESS

One of the first phrases we learn as children is "That's not fair!" The fairness concept is based on rules we humans have to live by, unless we want all outcomes to be dictated by bullies. The premise is that everybody has agreed to play by the rules. Maturing is the process of learning that everything does not go by the rules. Even parents—who live in a world of inequities and unfairness and know that their children will eventually have to make their ways in such a world—persist in settling playground disputes and dealing with household dilemmas on the basis of what is fair.

Life gives us repeated examples of bad things happening to good people and good things happening to bad people. Yet, we continue assuming that the fairness concept is true. We jump to our feet in the courtroom of life and shout, "I object! This is not fair!"

But maybe we are not talking about fairness at all. Maybe "it's not fair" is just a phrase that pops out of our mouths when we more accurately ought to be saying that we just don't like what has happened, or that what has happened does not seem appropriate from our viewpoint.

We question the fairness when a young person dies. "She had her whole life ahead of her! How unfair for her to die so young." Pain accompanies all losses, but it can be especially intense and vivid when a loved one dies prematurely, suddenly, violently—or all of the above.

At such times, our questions about fairness are certainly understandable and legitimate.

In truth, however, death is neither fair nor unfair. It just is. What we object to is the timing of a death, and that this loss involved us ("Why me? Why now?"). But think about it for a moment—how often do we complain about the timing when something good happens to us? How often do we respond, "This is not fair. I just don't deserve for this good thing to happen to me now"?

As for "Why me?" questions, think about this: earthquakes, tornadoes, and other tragedies happen all the time to people who don't deserve them. Seldom do we hear ourselves saying, "It would have been fairer if that terrible thing had happened to my people than to the people in that story."

Do we need a system for grief like the one that measures earthquakes, so we could say, "Your tragedy measured four-point-nine on the Grief Scale but mine was a six-point-two"? Would that help us decide what's fair? We could say, "A grief experience of two-point-one is fair, but anything over that is unfair—unless you've been really bad!"

The more we mature, the more we realize how difficult it is to determine in advance which actions and events will have good outcomes and which will have bad ones. We sometimes jump to conclusions, as in the humorous story of the old farmer who reported that his horse had run away. The neighbors responded, "Oh, that's bad." "Actually not," said the farmer. "My son went after it and found another horse. So, we had two horses." The neighbors smiled, "Oh, that's good." "No," said the farmer. "When they started into our barn, the two horses crushed my son's leg against the barn door." "Oh, that's bad," said the neighbors. "Not really," said the farmer. "Because of his broken leg, my son was not taken into the army. So, he lived while many others died in the war." "Then, that's good,"

said the neighbors. "Not really," responded the farmer. "We lost the war and the
enemy came and took both my horses."
It's a story that never ends and is never
complete—just like our understanding of
what's good and bad, what's fair and
what's unfair.

As the great Jack Benny was accept-
ing a prestigious award, he is reported to
have said, "I really don't deserve this
award. But then, I have arthritis, and I
don't deserve that either."

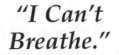

"I Can't Breathe."

(Physical Effects)

CHAPTER 3

CASE STUDY
The invisible boa constrictor

Lawanda hated to see her old friends coming. She knew they would ask, "How are you doing?" These people weren't going to settle for "Fine." They wanted the full story about Lawanda's recovery from the sudden, unexplained crib death of her beautiful Jamie. They weren't being nosy or suspicious. They were sincerely concerned for Lawanda.

Emotionally, spiritually, and physically, Lawanda was as low as she could go. She felt like a walking corpse. If she were to give them a full answer, she would have to listen to all their advice. These were loving, well-meaning friends, but Lawanda just needed time alone.

Eventually, she settled on the boa constrictor. When they asked how she was doing, Lawanda replied, "Well, I think I am making slow progress, but I would be a whole lot better if I didn't have an invisible boa constrictor wrapped around my lungs. I just can't get a full, deep breath."

It was an answer that worked for Lawanda. First of all, it was honest. Since the moment of Jamie's death, she had felt as if she were being crushed under a giant weight. She was physically weak. She had no energy. And she was as short of breath as her grandfather had been after his heart attack. It was an honest answer that shifted the topic away from little Jamie.

Most importantly, the image of the invisible boa constrictor opened the door and let Lawanda's friends into her life of grief. She was confiding in them. She was telling them how she really felt. But she was doing it in a way that let them clearly understand that she was too weak to stand and talk for very long.

In time, Lawanda was able to breathe normally again, despite her invisible boa constrictor. And her friends breathed easier, too, knowing where she was in her grief.

Discussion/Reflection Questions

1. *Why did Lawanda feel like she had a boa constrictor wrapped around her lungs? Was she really short of breath? Was the problem all in her mind?*

2. *What physical maladies sometimes strike people because of their emotional distress?*

3. *What similarities can you see between the psychological symptoms of grief and the physical symptoms when the body goes into shock?*

4. *Occasionally, computer experts find that they can solve problems by "taking the whole system down and bringing it back up." How does this resemble the body's reaction to grief?*

5. *What advice would you give to a person such as Lawanda about the physical manifestations of emotional pain?*

6. *In your opinion, does Lawanda need to see a doctor? Does she need to see a mental health professional?*

7. *If you had the power to magically cure Lawanda's shortness of breath on the spot, how do you think she might respond? Would she be grateful? Would she "miss" her shortness of breath or feel guilty about losing it?*

A few thoughts on
OUTWARD SIGNS OF INNER PAIN

My book *When There Are No Words* has a chapter entitled "Two Cement Blocks Ready to Wear." In it I try to describe the physical shortness of breath that attacked me after the sudden deaths of Tim and Don and Bryan [editor's note: see Chapter 12]. Reader response to that chapter has been very surprising. People who have been helped by the book often refer specifically to that chapter. It gave them words to describe a grief phenomenon that is quite common—but rarely articulated.

Whether you describe it as cement blocks on your chest or an invisible boa constrictor around your lungs, the feeling is real to many who have endured the physical symptoms of grief. After the death of someone you love, there is often a feeling that some invisible force is squeezing the life out of you.

In addition to loss of breath, physical

symptoms of emotional pain may show up as loss of appetite, loss of sexual interest, or loss of concentration. Some grievers experience functional amnesia. Their minds declare sit-down strikes or decide to move at only half speed while figuring out how to cope with the tragic new reality.

One reason the cement-block chapter seems to have encouraged so many people is that it assures them that their condition is temporary. With my normal breathing back, it is easy to look back and describe my shortness of breath in a light-hearted way. But while I was in the middle of that attack, it was frightening. When you don't know how long a physical result of emotional pain is going to last, when you fear that it could go on forever, it can multiply your grief many times over.

Once you know that physical manifestations of grief are completely normal and almost certainly temporary, it is possible to accept them as part of your grief work. They can even contain a blessing. Physical symptoms are out there where we can see them, measure them, and tell how fast they are healing. Invisible injuries that remain within our minds and spirits are much more difficult to deal with.

One woman told me about breaking her foot just before her husband died. "It turned out to be a blessing in disguise," she recalled. "It gave me a visible excuse to reduce my expectations of myself and let people do things for me. I might have tried to keep going at full speed through the grief, but I was willing to slow down for a broken foot."

CHAPTER 4

"I'm Finding Out Who My Real Friends Are."

(Friendship in Grief)

CASE STUDY
Coffee and sympathy

The man behind the counter came over with the pot and asked, "Ready for another refill?"

"No, Mark," Robert answered. "I'm really rolling on self-pity here, and I don't need more caffeine to pep me up while feeling bad is feeling so good."

Mark replaced the coffee pot. "Whatever you say, my friend. If anybody deserves a round of self-pity, it's you, man. Tell you the truth, I'm still suffering from what happened to you. Beats me how you are getting through it at all."

Robert took off his glasses and rubbed his itchy eyes. "No other choice but to get through it. Nothing I can do to bring that kid back to life. I hit the brakes all night long in my sleep, and I still can't stop the car fast enough to keep from hitting that kid. I tell myself I did everything I could, but I just keep seeing the little guy as they laid him out on the sidewalk. It's gonna take a lot of coffee to wash that picture away."

"Well, I can make the coffee. Just wish there was more I could do."

Robert stared at his coffee spoon. "You do a lot more than you know, Mark. You've been a real friend. A thing like this shows you who your real friends are. Some people I thought were friends came around early, said they were sorry, slapped me on the back, and disappeared for good. Now, if they see me coming, they go the other way."

Mark leaned against the counter. "Sometimes people just don't know what to say. I used to be a bartender. I learned that most folks don't want you to give them the answer. They just want you to listen."

"Exactly right, Mark. There is no solution. I just need them to stand by me while I'm stuck in the problem."

Discussion/Reflection Questions

1. *In what ways has Mark proven himself a true friend to the grieving Robert?*

2. *How might you respond if you were one of Robert's old friends and heard that he felt you had abandoned him in his grief?*

3. *Have you ever said (or written) to someone who was grieving, "If there is anything I can do to help, please ask"? Did you really mean it? Did they ask you to do anything? Have you ever just done something to help a grieving person, without waiting to be asked?*

4. *Sometimes grieving people are harder on*

*their friends than they would be otherwise.
Can you think of reasons why a person in
grief might be more demanding and less
forgiving than other people?*

5. *Explain the difference between "listening"
and "keeping quiet while you wait for your
chance to talk."*

6. *If you are familiar with the biblical story of
Job, you can probably explain the observation someone once made that "Job's three
friends were a great help to him—until
they started talking."*

7. *What assistance have you seen churches,
businesses, or other organizations offer to
members or employees who were grieving?
Can you think of other things that groups
could do that would help?*

A few thoughts on
FRIENDSHIP IN GRIEF

When you listen to people exchange

stories in grief support groups, it's never very long before the subject of friends comes up. Occasionally, you get to hear a happy story about the thoughtful and sensitive support of a good friend. More often, there is bitterness in the accounts you hear of abandonment, insensitive statements, and unrealistic expectations about recovery from grief.

Sometimes co-workers and associates of grieving people think that a gruff, matter-of-fact approach will help the victim leave the grief behind. They say things like, "Okay, Jones. Life has handed you a tough break, but you've got to put it all behind you and get on with your life. It's been two weeks now, and it's time for you to start pulling your part of the load again."

Otherwise intelligent people and devoted friends can be thoughtless when it comes to the words they choose to try to encourage those in grief. Some make the problem worse by trying to suggest reasons why this loss is not so bad after all. They say, "Fortunately, you're still young so you can have other children." Or, "At least you still have your health." Or, "Think of all the people in the world who are worse off than you are." Or the ever-popular, "It could have been a whole lot worse."

Equally hurtful for the person in grief is the friend who is so uncertain about saying or doing the wrong thing that he or she does nothing. Rather than choose the wrong words, they say no words at all. Rather than do the wrong thing, they never show up at all. They convince themselves that "probably some of the other friends who know the right things to do and say in this kind of situation have already stepped in and are doing the right things. I am not needed."

A person in grief needs most of all an honest friend who will come, and stay, and fumble, and make innocent mistakes, and confess to not knowing what to say or do, and hug, and cry, and be frustrated alongside the griever. The person may not have memorized *101 Encouraging Lines to Say to Persons in Grief.* The person may not have encountered the situation before. He or she may not have the answers. But the person will be there for you, and will tell you the truth.

We all need community. We need people we know well and can count on in adversity. Life traumas certainly reveal to us how close and committed our friends are, but we also have to realize that their lives and schedules were full long before our tragedy added extra responsibilities for them.

One of the greatest lessons of the grieving process is that there are two sides to every friendship, and in most cases you will receive the kind of friendship and support that you have given. A true friend will be three things when a life trauma occurs. The friend will be there. The friend will be listening. And the friend will be honest.

CHAPTER 5

"Make Decisions? In the Middle of All This?"

(Decision Making)

CASE STUDY
The car that wouldn't die

"Where are you going?" the mother asked.

"Frank is taking me to the lot where they impounded Cheryl's car," the father answered. "Someone called and said that we have to pick the car up by tomorrow or they start charging daily rent."

"Daily rent!" she frowned. "Don't they know what we've been through? Do they expect us to deal with that car so soon after...after the accident?"

"The girl who called knows nothing about the car," he responded. "She's just doing her job. I'll be back in a couple of hours."

"I don't want to ever see that car again," she said, staring out at the drizzling rain.

He closed the back door, stepped into weather that matched his mood, and fell into the front seat of Frank's car. "You sure you want to tend to this yourself?" asked Frank. "I can get someone else to drive it back here for you."

"No, it's gotta go someplace besides here," he said flatly. "The insurance expires in two weeks. Gotta make some decisions before that."

They rode in silence to the police department. The receptionist told him who was in charge at the lot. He showed his identification and the attendant produced the keys to Cheryl's car. Seeing the familiar good-luck charm on Cheryl's key chain almost did him in.

Tear-filled eyes kept him from reading the form he signed. He found the car, unlocked the door, got in, and adjusted the seat. When he turned the key, he was immediately surrounded by loud music from the tape player—Cheryl's music, the music she was listening to when she died.

The engine started on the first try. He was relieved. Last thing he wanted was to jump-start the car that took his daughter's life. He put the car in gear and it rolled slowly toward the gate. His foot on the accelerator brought the low, roaring sound of a faulty muffler.

"The way things are going," he thought to himself, "I'll get pulled over for a loud muffler. Okay, guys. Do what you have to do. It won't change the way my day is going."

He didn't get pulled over. He drove along the two-lane highway slowly, while irritated drivers passed him whenever they had the chance. He didn't notice them. He was lost in his thoughts. "The car can't go home. I'll have to renew the insurance if I don't get rid of it right away. I can't sell it without a new muffler. And getting a new muffler is just going to open up a whole new chain of decisions to be made."

His grip on the wheel tightened as he drove toward the horizon in the car that wouldn't die.

Discussion/Reflection Questions

1. *Should the grieving father have tried to deal with the car in which his daughter died? Why or why not?*

2. *What factors keep one's judgment from being completely sound after a life trauma?*

3. *How long should grieving people wait before they resume making important decisions?*

4. *What are some ways decisions could be therapeutic after a life trauma? Or harmful?*

5. *"Make no major decisions for a year after the death of a loved one,"* is a familiar piece of advice. How easy is it to follow this advice? What are some factors that make it very difficult to follow?

6. One man with a terminal illness realized that he had always handled all the details of the home and family. In his final months, he worked frantically to make sure his wife and children would not have to make any decisions after he died. Wise or unwise?

A few thoughts on DECISION-MAKING

When someone you love dies, you are emotionally overwhelmed. You need time to sit and grieve. If you are wise, you lower your expectations of yourself, reducing what you think you ought to be able to do physically, mentally, and emotionally. But eventually, someone trying to help you looks up from a stack of mail

you have ignored and asks, "Do you realize that if you don't pay your bill before
Thursday, they are going to cut off your
heat and electricity?"

Your grief response may well be
"Fine! Let 'em turn it off! I'll freeze in the
dark. Don't they make allowances for
human emergencies? I can't think about
things like that at a time like this."

While the grieving person would like
to shout, "Stop the world! I want off!"
there are some decisions that cannot be
avoided. Funeral details have to be handled. Some decisions can be delegated,
but eventually life's responsibilities must
be resumed, no matter how much we
wish we could leave them all behind.

There obviously is no simple answer
to the question of how long we should
allow ourselves to obey our grief before
we return to responsibilities. Some
employers would like to say, "In the
event of a death in the family, human
emotions require 17 days of recovery
time. Therefore, we expect you to be fully

ready to cope with life's demands on day 18." But humans don't work that way. The required time is different for every griever. Even when we do return to our daily functions, we need a gradual return instead of a simple switching of our minds from "off" to "on."

Part of the answer is letting other people do things for you. One woman told me, "If it hadn't been for my daughter and her husband, I would have probably ended up in jail after my husband died. Fortunately, they protected me from the decisions I might have made." Yet even with loving care-givers around, there comes a time when the person in grief has to begin to take hold again and resume the management of his or her own life.

Some people try to escape grief by jumping immediately into work responsibilities and occupying their minds with details. Sometimes it works, but often they are far less able to make clear decisions than they think they are.

Depression—which goes hand-in-hand with grief—is especially detrimental to clear decision making. Very few people have the luxury of taking off the ideal amount of time. Life makes its demands and rarely provides as much patience and understanding as our grief deserves.

CHAPTER 6

"I'm Okay. Don't Make a Fuss."

(Caring for the Bereaved)

CASE STUDY
The widow's monologue

"Life has not been easy since Roger died. He and I were married 47 years ago. You do more than get used to somebody in 47 years. You become one person, just like the Good Book says. So now I feel like half a person rattling around in this old place.

"I never realized how much of my life revolved around taking care of Roger, especially in the years since he retired. You get up in the morning and it's time to think about breakfast. When Roger was here, there was a reason for breakfast. Now, it's just me, and I'm not very hungry. Roger and I would eat breakfast and read the paper together, and I would always remind him to take his medicine. Now, I don't have to remind anybody to do anything, and reading the newspaper seems kind of useless when you do it all by yourself.

"We had a good life together. Worked hard. Raised four wonderful children. Never had a minute's trouble out of any of them. We have nine beautiful grand-children. We are—I mean, I am proud of each and every one of them. Only two of our children still live here in town but they are all real thoughtful about calling to check on how I'm doing.

"They haven't forgotten me like the children of some of my friends have. They drive over here on weekends. They are always doing repairs around the house for me. They even check my cabi-nets when they come, and then they go buy groceries for me.

"I do appreciate their concern but I

tell them not to make a fuss over me. They have their own lives and they all stay just as busy as can be running here and there. I tell them that I am still able to get around and do for myself, though I just don't have the interest in doing a lot of the things I used to do when Roger was here. I feel kind of like a sailboat when the wind stops blowing—I can still float but there's not much to make me go.

"It does take the wind out of your sails when you lose half of who you are—maybe more than half in my case. I know I'm going to be all right here. And I do appreciate the way the children keep trying to do things for me, but I keep telling them, 'I'm okay. Don't make a fuss.'"

Discussion/Reflection Questions

1. *Did you hear any statements in the widow's monologue that make you think she might be deceiving herself?*

2. *If this widow confided these feelings and concerns to you, what would be your advice to her?*

3. *What difference would it make if the widow were saying these words three months after Roger's death or three years after his death?*

4. *In your opinion, are the widow's children doing a positive thing or a negative thing by being so attentive to their mother's needs?*

5. *Do grievers need help from others? Do they want help from others? What can be done to make it easier for people to ask for help when they need it?*

6. *Have you known of cases where people used grief to turn others into their servants?*

7. *Does it sound like this widow will create a*

new life for herself, or simply pine away in loneliness?

A few thoughts on
CARING FOR THE BEREAVED

When trauma strikes, people need differing amounts of help and support. Some people have more independent spirits than others, but all of us need to know that help and support have been offered. Even if you are going to graciously decline offers of assistance, your self-image and your ability to weather your grief depend a lot on knowing that others care what happens to you—care enough to interrupt their busy schedules and do things for you.

When we say, "Don't make a fuss," we may be communicating a number of different messages. Some of us are actually saying, "Do make a fuss over me. I am in trouble here. I don't really know what I am doing. This grief has me so totally baffled that, while I feel it is polite to say 'don't make a fuss,' I desperately hope that you will continue to help me to do things I am not yet able to do for myself."

Another message underlying "Don't make a fuss" could be, "I am embarrassed about having to accept your help. I have always taken pride in the fact that I've never had to ask anybody for anything. Surrendering that pride is difficult. Whether I truly need your help or not, I feel the need to register my discomfort with the words 'Don't make a fuss.'"

Finally, those same words may mean exactly what they say. The person may quite honestly and accurately be communicating, "While I am appreciative of your eagerness to be of service, and while I recognize the love and affection that prompts your actions in my behalf, I feel that I have gotten past the hardest parts of this grief journey and will be able to tend to these needs on my own. I do want to stay in touch, and your continuing friendship is very important to my continued recovery."

When dealing with a person who is grieving, we must remember that words can mean a wide variety of things. We are often victims of social constraints and fears that keep us from speaking our minds, even to those closest to us. Each of us should be dedicated to building friendships in which we can freely speak the truth. We need to develop friends to whom we can say, "Look, I am hurting a lot. I can't manage. But I know I can turn to you for help."

"Don't Talk to Me About God."

(Faith and Grief)

CHAPTER 7

CASE STUDY
Where was God?

Gerald was a boy who loved to play. Even when everyone else was serious, Gerald seemed to be able to find the humorous side of the situation. Sometimes people liked this characteristic, thinking that Gerald was good at bringing cheer into even the most hopeless situation. At other times, people were irritated that Gerald never seemed to take things seriously. Some wondered if Gerald's comedy act was a mask to keep him from having to deal with serious things that made him uncomfortable.

When the news spread that Gerald had died of a self-inflicted gunshot, everyone's grief was mixed with confusion. Some were asking, "How could such a happy-go-lucky kid commit suicide?" Others were saying, "I knew all along that his playfulness was hiding deep emotional troubles and fears."

The police investigation confused things even more. Gerald had not seemed depressed to those who were with him in the hours before he died. He had even made plans with a friend for the next day. And there was no ammunition clip in the gun that took Gerald's life. Gerald probably had no idea that a single bullet was lurking inside the gun. It would have been fully in character for him to be "play-acting" a suicide with what he assumed to be an unloaded gun. But suddenly the playfulness was deadly serious.

It was a freak accident. If that renegade shell hadn't been there, there would have been no accident. If friends had been present, the accident probably would not have happened. Like most accidents, this one could have been avoided by different behavior. But like many accidents, the behavior was only known to be dangerous after it was too late.

Was God there? Was God watching as Gerald played unknowingly with a loaded gun? Was God willing to watch as the bullet exploded and ended the boy's life? Did God know how much pain would be suffered by so many people when this young giver of smiles left the earth? Did God know all this and still let it happen? Was God teaching somebody a lesson, letting events take their own course, or just busy somewhere else in the universe? Or what?

Discussion/Reflection Questions

1. *In your opinion, what was God's role in Gerald's death? Did God allow it? Cause it? Have nothing to do with it? Is there*

another way to understand it?

2. *Would your opinions about God's involvement in this accidental death be different if Gerald had been your own brother?*

3. *What are some of the reasons that people in grief so often get mad at God?*

4. *What things that can be agitating to those in grief might well-intentioned people say about God's place in all of this?*

5. *Sometimes the death of a friend or family member can change a person's entire relationship with God. Grief can drive a person away from God or toward God. What examples of this have you observed?*

6. *Brainstorm the implications of a world in which no one died. How would life be different for you and the people around you if there were no such thing as death?*

7. *There is an old saying: "A God who was*

*simple enough for us to understand would
not be complex enough to meet our needs."
Do you agree or disagree? What value does
such a concept have to a grieving person
who is angry at God?*

8. *When a person in grief asks, "Where was
God when this terrible thing happened,"
are they asking for an answer or could
there be some other purpose for asking the
question?*

A few thoughts about
FAITH AND GRIEF

Persons in grief naturally gravitate to
the question of why the thing happened
that is causing the pain. For those who
believe in God, there is often a great
struggle involved in resolving the question of why an all-powerful Creator, who
claims in sacred writings to love his creatures, would cause or even allow bad
things to happen to those creatures. The
answers don't come easily—partly

because we mix so many of our own assumptions about the situation in with the question, and partly because we humans are just naturally reluctant to discover answers we don't like, or answers that contradict popular attitudes about God.

Even people who rarely think about God from day to day find themselves face to face with the question of whether some super-human, external force (they may call it God, providence, karma, fate, destiny, or fortune) might have brought about the otherwise inexplicable event that is causing them grief. And the "follow-up question" is even tougher than the first one: *"If my chosen super-human, external force did this to me, what did I do to deserve it? And what is it that I am supposed to do to get back in good standing with this spiritual bully so that no more bad stuff comes my way?"*

There are some in our world who have long ago considered and dismissed the possibility that *any* outside force alters, shapes, influences, or directs the events of human existence. Do such people have an easier time in grief situations? Do atheists face fewer dilemmas in times of grief?

When we hear persons in grief situations say, "Don't talk to me about God at a time like this," it is probably another case of people not saying exactly what they mean, using one set of well-worn words when they really mean to communicate something else altogether. They are saying, "Don't talk to me about God." They really intend to communicate, "Don't start telling me a lot of stuff about the relationship that you have worked out with your God. I am very busy at the moment mulling over how this tragic event fits with, and may change or expand, my own way of thinking about God."

Every grief encounter is an opportunity to grow as a person, especially as a spiritual person. For all the negatives of pain and anguish, there is positive value in the kinds of thoughts that such events force us to think—the basic life values and relationships we are forced to consider and reconsider. As one wise mother expressed it, "When my son was born healthy, I never asked *why*. But since he became seriously ill, I have not stopped asking *why*."

As we struggle with questions of faith in the face of loss and grief, it is comforting to remember that there can be no faith without doubt. When you respect your doubts, you are respecting your faith.

CHAPTER 8

"I Think I May Be Losing My Mind."

(Psychological Effects)

CASE STUDY
The evidence is quite conclusive

All her life, Allison had joked about losing her mind. Now she seriously believed the joking was over. Allison's teenagers had always laughed when she would muss her hair and make a wild face as she said, "Teenagers are driving me up the wall! You kids are making me stark raving bonkers!"

Kim especially had loved her mom's comedic way of lightening the heavy interactions between parent and child. But Kim was no longer present to notice the difference. A driver with a brain full of alcohol had crossed the center line and crashed head-on into Kim's car as she drove home from cheerleading practice.

Kim's funeral was now two weeks past, but Allison was still conversing with her daughter. She would sit in Kim's room for hours, slowly turning the pages of Kim's scrapbook and whispering things like, "Wasn't that a great birthday party, Kimmy? You looked so cute in that dress I made for you. And you were so excited when your birthday present barked before you could even unwrap the box."

Now Allison sits and holds that birthday present. Sparky licks her tears, knowing something is wrong. And Allison squeezes the little dog too tightly and scares them both.

It's not just talking to the dog, and to herself, and to her absent daughter that worries Allison. She can also tell that she is becoming very forgetful. She wanders into a room of the house and stands there, trying to remember what she came there to do. She stares at page after page of a book without knowing a single word she has read. Driving home, Allison suddenly realizes that, even in her own neighborhood, she has absolutely no idea where she is or how to get home.

Allison always took pride in her appearance. Now she sees no reason to put on makeup or fix her hair. Going out of the house is filled with painful reminders of Kim. Allison may suddenly break into tears at the grocery store because of memories sparked by a simple can of creamed corn. At church, many of the old hymns seem to mention death more than they did before.

Even good friends who approach Allison intending to say a word of comfort sometimes appear to her as nightmarish faces with mouths moving but no sound coming out. The evidence seems conclusive to Allison. She thinks she is losing her mind. Maybe she is.

Discussion/Reflection Questions

1. *What is your diagnosis? Is Allison losing her mind? If not, what other explanation can you give?*

2. *If this is only temporary, what would be your advice to Allison about getting through it?*

3. *What mind-bending effects of grief have you experienced yourself or observed in others?*

4. *Does there seem to be a specific amount of time after which mental powers return to normal?*

5. *Is the fear of going crazy limited only to those who may have suffered the death of a loved one? Have you noted psychological effects that stem from other, less severe grief situations?*

6. *Can you think of reasons that people commonly fear for their sanity during grief? Are there reasons some grievers might even wish they were losing their minds?*

A few thoughts about the
PSYCHOLOGICAL EFFECTS OF
GRIEF

The support group has become a fixture in our world. After the pioneering success of Alcoholics Anonymous, support groups have sprung up for any and all of life's maladies. Support groups proliferate because they work. It makes a positive difference to sit in a circle and listen to imperfect strangers relate sad stories that are similar to yours.

It is not that we feel better because we go to support groups and meet so many people who are suffering as we are. It is not that we feel better because we win some kind of morbid competition for having the saddest story of all. The positive therapy of any support group is perspective—discovering that we are not alone.

If your leg is amputated, no one can sympathize and encourage like a person who has also lost a leg. If you stutter, have a gambling addiction, have breast cancer, it helps to meet a person who has been there. As you battle to describe the confusion and frustration you are feeling, their knowing expressions and understanding nods tell you that your words are making absolute sense to someone.

Some of the most inspirational moments at meetings of The Compassionate Friends or other support groups for those who have lost loved ones occur when first-timers confess that they sincerely fear that they may be going crazy. Instead of suspicious stares, support group members are likely to respond, "Been there. Done that." Or, "Yes, I remember the feeling well." Or, "You wouldn't be normal if you didn't think you were going crazy. It's going to take a while, but you will be fine."

One of my friends has written of a syndrome that she has humorously dubbed BBD, for Bereavement Brain Damage. Her descriptions of absent-minded behaviors and unfocused thinking are humorous to those whose life traumas are in the past, and encouraging to those who are still in the early stages of grief.

BBD is a natural condition for grieving persons, and also remarkably similar to the recognized scientific condition of Post-Traumatic Stress Disorder. The causes are similar. Whether it is a naive youngster from a secure home plunged into jungle combat, or parents learning from a policeman that their baby has died, the result is the same. They face sudden and disorienting horrors that are completely outside their previous frames of reference. They experience traumatic stress.

When grief strikes, the mind automatically goes into emergency mode. It initiates a process of keeping you physically alive while you endure an emotional shock like none you have ever experienced. Like the emergency program of a huge power plant, your mind is masterfully programmed to take off line some of your ancillary systems until your life-sustaining systems have dealt with the initial challenge. With parts of your brain on temporary leave, it is quite normal to assume that you are going insane.

Eventually, as your mind begins to sense that your life has passed the crisis and been sustained, it gradually and systematically brings your other faculties back on line. It is a truly inspired system, designed to protect us. Don't be alarmed to notice it at work in the midst of your own grief. You are not going crazy. You are grieving.

"Like a Cut on Your Little Finger."

(All-Inclusiveness of Grief)

CHAPTER 9

CASE STUDY
That Howard has a way

A few weeks after the death of his father, Howard said to me, "You know, my father's death reminds me of a cut on my little finger."

I waited for him to say more. But Howard wasn't worrying about making sense. He trusted me as a friend. He knew he was free to ramble, speak his mind, and surface the thoughts that boiled within.

After a moment, I said, "Howard, you've got me fascinated and confused with 'my father's death is like a cut on my little finger.' I know you don't mean it's inconsequential, because I've seen the depth of your pain these last few weeks."

Howard held up his little finger in front of me. He turned it around. Finally, he said, "How often do you think about your little finger? Not very. As long as that little guy is in good shape and doing his job, you never think about him. But then you get a cut on your little finger, and what happens? Every move you make reminds you of that little finger. You grab something with that hand and the pain zooms up to your brain, saying, 'Hey! Watch it! There's a hurt finger here!' Or you reach into your pocket for something and that sore makes you slow down and remember your little finger. You get into a hot shower and suddenly your thoughts are focused on your little finger."

"You're saying," I ventured, "that everything reminds you of your dad?"

"Exactly," said Howard, looking past me with misty eyes. "Dad was a part of my life. But as long as he was alive and well, I rarely gave him a thought. Had anyone asked, I would have told them how much I appreciated him. But no one was asking. Now, every little thing that happens reminds me of him. I get in the car and I hear him teaching me how to drive when I was 15. I look at a menu and I see foods he liked and didn't like. I get a headache and I remember how he lived with pain for so many years. I hear his words coming out of my mouth. No matter what I do, it reminds me of my dad."

Now, the mist from Howard's eyes was in my eyes. "Thanks for sharing your thoughts, my friend," I said. "I'll never think about a cut on my finger in the same way again."

Discussion/Reflection Questions

1. *Have you found Howard's observation about the cut on the little finger to be true of grief you have experienced? What were*

*some of the things that reminded you of
your loss?*

2. *One mother told of the troubling
reminders of her son in the first months
after his death. "Every part of the daily
routine, everything I did, reminded me of
him," she recalled. Would you consider
this a help or a hindrance in getting
through grief?*

3. *There is a saying that "A kid with a new
hammer thinks everything is a nail." Have
you seen grief so completely take over a
person's life that everything points to the
tragedy?*

4. *The passage of time eventually heals cuts
on little fingers. Does it work that way
with grief?*

A few words about the
ALL-INCLUSIVENESS OF GRIEF

It is impossible to be in two places at

one time. It is impossible to be in the
midst of the first crushing moments of
your life trauma and simultaneously be
months or years into your recovery.
Would it help if those of us who try to
encourage you could convince you that
someday things would be all right again?

In my opinion, it would not help. A
person who is at ground zero of a life
trauma needs to spend time in that exact
location. That person needs to feel the
hopelessness and frustration. That person
needs to react in natural ways to the
unwelcome change, the dreaded readjust-
ments, the absolute impossibility of seeing how life can possibly go forward
from the shattered present. The person
needs a little time to believe that all is
lost, that the worst has occurred, and that
there may be no future.

Later, grievers need to deal with the
painful reminders that pop up to con-
front them with their loss. Grief recovery
could be defined in part as having longer
and longer spaces between your

moments of vivid awareness of your loss.
But no matter how long it has been since
your loss, jolts of awareness are going to
occur. When they do, they will return
you abruptly to the same shock you
experienced when you first experienced
the loss. You had momentarily forgotten,
you had begun to think everything was
all right. Now a reminder jerks you back
to the moment the pain began.

Well-meaning friends bring platitudes
and casseroles to try to short circuit your
moaning and crying. You still have to
fully experience your grief. Ancient soci-
eties, with their hired weepers and wail-
ers and their recognized periods of
lamentation, were certainly more in tune
with the natural human requirements of
grieving than is our driven society, where
we encourage people to "shake it off,"
"put it behind you," "look on the bright
side," and "play through the pain."

Grief gives us new perspective on life.
We see relationships that were never
obvious before. We miss things that we

assumed would always be ours. We re-appraise the things we value. Good results can come from events we hate. They can mature us. They can make us wiser. Over time, good can come out of bad.

But the lessons of grief can be lost if we keep changing the subject, diverting our attention, avoiding the obvious, and fleeing the pain. Whatever tragedy has happened to you, you owe it to your-self—to your present and your future, to your growth and development, to your honesty and self-respect—to plum the depths of its pain. Don't run from it; experience it. Listen to its lessons. Be reminded. Accept every jab of its pain. You never get over pain that you don't allow yourself to feel.

"What Do You Mean, 'Life Goes On'?"

(Depression)

CHAPTER 10

CASE STUDY
Cardboard for breakfast

"I think I know you well enough to tell you honestly what I am thinking. We have been through enough of life's bumps and scrapes together that I know you're not going to fly into denial when I say that I see absolutely no purpose for me to go on living.

"Ever since the funeral, my life is just bland, meaningless, empty. I am too much of a coward to do anything in the way of suicide, but lots of nights when I fall into bed, I wish that I just wouldn't wake up the next morning.

"Actually, I feel ashamed to be surrendering to depression, because I know the world is full of people who have real reasons to be depressed. There are people starving, people with terminal illnesses. And here I am—no real financial problems, friends who are concerned about me—and I just don't care if the sun comes up tomorrow.

"You know how I picture my life these days? It's like I get up every morning and sit down at a breakfast table, and there before me is a big bowl of shredded cardboard. You know, you can eat cardboard if you chew it long enough, ignore the fact that it tastes awful, and just keep plugging through it, one tasteless piece at a time.

"That's the way a day looks to me— like eating a large bowl of cardboard. Each thing I have to do at work, each conversation I have, each task of the day, is just another piece of cardboard that has to be chewed until I can swallow it. Sometimes, if I soak a piece in rum, it's a little easier to get down. Or maybe there's a drop of honey to make the cardboard go down. But all in all, that's the way life feels to me. Get out of bed and start chewing through another bowl of cardboard.

"And if there is one thing that really pushes me to the brink, it is when people try to cheer me up by saying, 'Well, life must go on!' It makes me want to say, 'Who says life has to go on? Why do I have to keep chewing my way through these tasteless days when my real purpose for living has been taken away from me?'"

Discussion/Reflection Questions

1. *Have you ever felt as hopeless as the person who delivered this monologue? What caused you to feel that way?*

2. *What advice would you give to the person who delivered this monologue?*

3. *Do you recall times when you thought your life was bad and would never get better, and then it did get better? What changed?*

4. *How natural a part of grief is depression? If someone you care for is depressed over a life trauma, what can you, as a friend, do for him or her?*

5. *Do you agree or disagree with the one-liner about depression: "You have to go through it to get to the other side of it"?*

6. *Since medical science now has medications called antidepressants, why should anyone still be depressed?*

7. *How do you know when to offer advice for your friend's problem and when to stress the need for professional counseling? Have you seen amateur advice backfire?*

8. *What should you do when depression talk includes mention of suicide?*

A few thoughts about
THE DEPRESSION OF GRIEF

Depression is what happens when there is no way to accomplish what we want, or, in some cases, no socially acceptable way to accomplish what we want. If we have goals that can be reached by working harder, we can usually harness the energy of our desires into greater and greater effort. No matter how slow the progress, we can keep plugging toward our goal as long as there appears to be even the faintest path between us and our objective, and even the slightest bit of progress. But once a goal we desperately desire appears to be impossible to reach, frustration hardens into depression and our ability to see our situation objectively dissolves into distorted views and irrational probabilities.

Life traumas are natural catalysts for frustration and depression. The characteristic that creates the grief also creates the frustration. Someone has died. We desperately want that person to be alive again, but there is no way.

People who have suffered a life trauma are often effective counselors for those in the midst of that trauma. This is because they know how useless it is to try and talk anybody out of depression. Telling someone the reasons why they should not be depressed is like putting out a campfire by pouring gasoline on it. The talk is wasted and may even accelerate the depression. Only the passage of time can dull the ache and ease the pain. As life proceeds, it will gradually supply its own reasons for continuation, but to tell a grieving person that life must go on is counterproductive.

On the other hand, it may not be necessary to eat the "entire bowl of cardboard." The idea that the only way to get to the other side of depression is to grit your teeth and slog through every painful inch of it may have been true years ago. But today, there are modern therapies and antidepressant medications

that can minimize the depression experience. They can be very helpful for those
who are willing to give them a try.

Sometimes, however, the fear of being
dependent that may have launched the
depression can also keep a person from
trying therapies or medications that
could help. It's not unusual to hear a
depressed person say, "I don't want to be
dependent on drugs. I should be able to
beat this thing on my own."

In the case of grief-caused depression,
there is an especially delicate balance to
be considered. Professional therapies and
medications can reduce the depth or
extent of depression, but they should not
be allowed to completely eliminate the
depression that is a natural part of healing. A certain amount of emotional frustration and depression belong in the normal grief-recovery process. To eliminate
them completely would be to steal part
of the natural tribute the griever is pay-
ing to the one who has died.

Depression is a natural part of grief, a

part that needs to be experienced; but grief-spawned depression need not last forever.

"When Does It Stop Hurting?"

(Long-Term Grief)

CHAPTER 11

CASE STUDY
I've never hurt this way before

"This is not like anything I have ever known before. It's pain, but not really physical pain. I've had broken bones and I have been through labor, and I would trade this for either of those, because at least you know those are going to end eventually. With this, I don't know. It seems to get worse instead of better. It comes in waves. For a while, the hurt is bearable. Then it hurts unbearably, and I think I am going to die.

"I guess I'd say it's more like a head-to-toe emotional ache than anything else—like the sword through the heart that I have seen in a few ancient religious paintings. When I am able to be at home alone, I give myself permission to go with the pain, to give it free rein, to think the thoughts that make it hurt even more. It is as if I want it to hurt worse and worse, so that when it finally eases, it will feel good.

"But there are other times when I just can't let it get a foothold. I have to stop it before it takes over my mind. At bedtime, I just can't let the thoughts begin that will steal the rest I need so much. I play mind games. I think about a scene from a book that I enjoyed a lot. I think through the dialogue. I remember that this character said *this*. And the other character responded with *this*. Back and forth, I reconstruct and replay the dialogue in my mind. It is enough of a mental challenge to hold the door against the thoughts I fear. It is enough mental exercise to tire me into the sleep I need so much.

"Once asleep, I only have to guard my dreams, to keep the faces I fear out of the movies of my mind. It is a constant battle. And sometimes, I am afraid that even if I win the battle, I will lose the war. If I keep tricking my pain so that it never gets to escape, it may build up inside me until my brain explodes."

Discussion/Reflection Questions

1. *This is one person's attempt to describe the pain she felt during grief. How do you feel about her habit of tricking her mind, at times, to escape the pain?*

2. *To what would you compare the pain your grief has caused you to experience?*

3. *Is it possible to go through a life trauma and feel no pain? If this were to happen, would it suggest something lacking in the person to whom it happened?*

4. *How long do you recall the pain of grief*

lasting for you? Did it stop abruptly or gradually? Do you remember what first made you realize that the pain was beginning to ease?

5. Do you think grief would be easier to deal with if every human being grieved in exactly the same way?

6. What advice would you give to a close friend who is facing the pain of grief?

7. One of the oldest descriptions of grief involves the term "broken heart." What strengths and weaknesses can you see in this way of describing emotional pain?

A few words about LONG-TERM GRIEF

One of my most uncomfortable moments is when I go to a meeting of parents whose children have died, and they divide us into small groups and it's time for each person in the circle to explain the event that brought him or her to the meeting. I have no reluctance or lack of words for telling my story. My discomfort results from the fact that my tragedy happened so many years ago.

As the sad stories are told, the times that most of the deaths occurred seem to fall into the range of "two weeks ago" to "three years ago." There are very few long-timers like me. Only rarely do I hear anyone else say that their child died over ten years ago.

My great discomfort results from the expressions on the faces of the others in the circle when I say how long it has been for me. There are obvious questions in their eyes. "Do you mean that it has been that long ago and you're still not over it yet?" Or they ask, "Are you telling me that I am going to continue hurting like this for that long?" Or they want to know, "Since you seem relatively at peace as you retell your story, what are you doing here? Why haven't you given up this group and gone back to the real world?" And at the heart of all their questions is the most natural curiosity for persons in pain. They want to know, "When does it stop hurting?"

Those parents are still suffering the physical and mental effects of grief shock. They can't catch their breaths. They have no appetites. Bodily functions are out of step. Mental functions are scrambled. They are disoriented. They cannot focus their minds. And more than anything else, they just hurt.

Their first curiosity is whether they are going to feel this bad permanently. They probably wouldn't be surprised if the answer were yes. They are still immersed in the all-pervasive event that has engulfed everything they know and value. They cannot imagine that life can ever return to what it was like before.

The question they are too polite to ask is the question that bothers me the most. A voice inside my own head keeps insinuating, "If you are not hurting now like you did at first, then maybe you don't still love Tim and Don as much as you did when they first died."

And so, I spend time answering a question that nobody has asked. "I am here after all these years because these meetings provide a regular time during which I can focus totally on my two sons who died. I am here to listen more than to talk, to share your pain and tell you a little about the long-term. I can tell you that the hurting will never stop, but there will be longer spaces between your bouts of pain. Even after many years, you can expect sudden reminders to plunge you back into the same pain you felt the moment you first received the news. I am here to tell you that the hurting never stops, it just takes a different form."

"How This Book Came to Be."

(The Personal Face of Grief)

CHAPTER 12

Our expedition into the valley of the shadow of death began before dawn on a cold December 15th. Kay and I stood in our den, sleepy-eyed and staring at a county policeman with an air of routine business about him.

The policeman looked down at his clipboard. "Do you have a son named Timothy Charles Walton?"

"Yes."

"Do you have a son named Donald Wayne Walton?"

"Yes."

"They are both dead."

We gasped. Kay sagged on my right arm. My mouth and throat were immediately dry and the first question that came to my mind emerged in a rasping voice. "What happened?"

The policeman did not change his monotone. "We don't know for sure. We think it might be a combination of things. They were found in a black Audi less than a mile from here. There were no signs of foul play. And there was another person with them."

The other person turned out to be Bryan, for 17 years Don's best friend and almost as much a part of our family as our own boys.

Thus began the second half of our life. Thus occurred the event that has caused all events of our family history to be categorized as happening "before the boys died" or "after the boys died." Thus began the series of events that have shown me that you can survive whatever news has shaken your world to its very foundations.

If you are going to live, you are going to face grief. It's what you get for loving.

Someone dies and leaves you with the most monumental lump of pain and fear you've ever seen. And if the death is sudden, your lump of grief comes with the added insult of shock, outrage, and disbelief. When Tim and Don were subtracted from my family of five, the impact was roughly equivalent to having two-fifths of my body surgically removed.

At the beginning of your grief, you are likely to be surrounded by well-meaning family and friends. They intend to help but they also have the option of drifting away if you grieve longer than they expect, or grieve in ways they don't expect. You, on the other hand, do not have the option of walking away. You are stuck with the job of long-term recovery. Different friends will help you through different parts of it. Kay and I were blessed with a church family that stayed the course, that extended its expressions of love and concern throughout the years of recovery—even to this day.

We survived the phenomenon called

grief. And, as the years passed, we realized that when we would go to talk with others who had been plunged into grief, our words seemed to actually make a difference. What we had learned was of help to hurting people. I began to think that what we had learned should be put into some form that could travel farther than we could. That's when I wrote *When There Are No Words,* a small and simple book designed for those who are in the first numbing weeks and months of grief. The response to that first book continues to be very gratifying.

When There Are No Words helped, and the conversations which arose from its acceptance made it clear to me that our death-denying culture needed to talk more honestly and more frequently about the way each one of our lives will end. Those conversations resulted in a second book, *Packing for the Big Trip,* to help people gain the major life benefits that come with increased awareness of death. Both books were published by Pathfinder

Publishing of California. They continue to bring aid to those in grief. Nothing in my life is quite as satisfying as getting to meet or hear from persons who have been helped by something I have written.

Those two books brought opportunities to meet many hurting persons, to listen to many stories, to share many frustrations, to pray for the lessening of many burdens. Those opportunities to speak and to listen added to my fascination with grief, a phenomenon that enters every life, but about which we rarely talk honestly.

Twelve Faces of Grief resulted from hours of participation in grief support groups. It is designed as a tool for those who seek to help, as well as those who seek help.

It is a resource for those who know that grief does not yield to "cures," but does mellow through discussion, exploration, and understanding. Nothing that I know of is quite as therapeutic to grieving persons as the sudden realization that they are not alone in this terrible experience.

Once the manuscript was written, a wide variety of group leaders, class participants, and close friends provided feedback to help improve the various stories and chapters. With deep gratitude, but also a wish to protect their privacy, I list their first names here, in alphabetical order by their unlisted last names. They provided their input with the understanding that this book's mission would be to serve those enduring the universal, yet one-of-a-kind, pain of grief. It is my hope and prayer that this book fulfills that purpose for you, dear reader, and eases your pain.

Thanks to Hubert, Jean, Eric, Marianna, Don, Susan, Paul, Ellen, Loretta, Gloria, Jeanie, Don, Butch, Charlene, Debbi, Kreg, Ric, Dave, Janice, Doris, Sondra, Newt, Jan, Richard, Beverly, Donna, Ed, James, Bob, Suzanne, Tony, Betty, Janice, Joe, Barbara, George, Doris, Gene, June, Alice, Alan, Lanita,

Gail, Louis, Bridget, Dena, Lester,
Marshall, Sharon, Pat, Marsha, Sharon,
Jimmy, Mary, Jim, Marsy, Shelia, Jean,
Paul, Suzie, Porter, Virginia, Diane,
Darlene, Freeman, Kathryn, Tony, Nancy,
Eric, Gene, Gerry, Hazel, Mary, Sybil,
Robert, Dick, Margaret, Chris, Sandee,
Bill, Hazel, Holly, Jerry, Susy, Mike, Lyn,
Margaret, Nonni, Rusty, Charm, Suzann,
Lee, Janice, Janice, Greg, Sally, Charles,
Diane, Beverly, Bob, Robin, Janet, Ross,
John, Susan, Ed, Joyce, Dottie, Jim, Vida,
Kay, Teresa, Mark, Bill, Sandy, Jim,
Tommy, Peggy, and Tom.